BIGGEST NAMES IN SPORTS

LEBRON JAMES

by Hubert Walker

BASKETBALL STAR

T0014854

FOCUS READERS
NAVIGATOR

WWW.FOCUSREADERS.COM

Focus Readers is distributed by North Star Editions:
sales@northstareditions.com | 888-417-0195

Produced for Focus Readers by Red Line Editorial.

Photographs ©: Mark J. Terrill/AP Images, cover, 1; Marcio Jose Sanchez/AP Images, 4–5; Tony Dejak/AP Images, 7; Eric Risberg/AP Images, 9; iStockphoto, 10–11; Icon Sportswire, 13; Jody Grigg/Ai Wire Photo Service/Newscom, 15; Mark Duncan/AP Images, 16–17; J. Pat Carter/AP Images, 19; Mark Humphrey/AP Images, 21; David Santiago/El Nuevo Herald/AP Images, 22–23; Mark Halmas/Icon Sportswire, 25; Chris Szagola/AP Images, 27; Red Line Editorial, 29

Library of Congress Cataloging-in-Publication Data
Names: Walker, Hubert, 1980- author.
Title: LeBron James : basketball star / by Hubert Walker.
Description: Lake Elmo, MN : Focus Readers, 2021. | Series: Biggest names in sports | Includes index. | Audience: Grades 4-6
Identifiers: LCCN 2020033634 (print) | LCCN 2020033635 (ebook) | ISBN 9781644937006 (hardcover) | ISBN 9781644937365 (paperback) | ISBN 9781644938089 (pdf) | ISBN 9781644937723 (ebook)
Subjects: LCSH: James, LeBron,--Juvenile literature. | Basketball players--United States--Biography--Juvenile literature. | African American basketball players--Biography--Juvenile literature.
Classification: LCC GV884.J36 W34 2021 (print) | LCC GV884.J36 (ebook) | DDC 796.323092 [B]--dc23
LC record available at https://lccn.loc.gov/2020033634
LC ebook record available at https://lccn.loc.gov/2020033635

Printed in the United States of America
Mankato, MN
012021

ABOUT THE AUTHOR

Hubert Walker enjoys running, hunting, and going to the dog park with his best pal. He grew up in Georgia but moved to Minnesota in 2018. Overall, he loves his new home, but he's not a fan of the cold winters.

TABLE OF CONTENTS

CHAPTER 1

BRINGING HOME A TITLE

LeBron James and the Cleveland Cavaliers were facing **elimination**. Cleveland trailed the Golden State Warriors three games to one in the 2016 National Basketball Association (NBA) Finals. To claim the title, the Cavs would have to win three straight games in the best-of-seven series.

LeBron James attempts a layup during the 2016 NBA Finals between the Cleveland Cavaliers and the Golden State Warriors.

Unfortunately for Cavs fans, history was not on their side. No team had ever come back from a 3–1 deficit in the Finals. To make matters worse, Game 5 took place in Oakland, California. That meant the Cavs would be playing in front of 19,000 screaming Warriors fans.

Few people expected Cleveland to come out on top. But James wasn't ready for his season to end. In Game 5, he put up 41 points. Teammate Kyrie Irving scored 41 points of his own. The Cavs cruised to a 112–97 victory.

The series moved to Cleveland, Ohio, for Game 6. Cavs fans packed the arena. They cheered their team to a

James drives on Stephen Curry of the Warriors during Game 6 of the 2016 NBA Finals.

115–101 win. Once again, James scored 41 points. The series was now tied 3–3. But the Cavaliers still had their work cut out for them. Game 7 took place back in Oakland.

Cleveland and Golden State were locked in a hard-fought battle. Game 7 was tied 89–89 with less than two minutes remaining. Andre Iguodala and Stephen Curry of the Warriors raced toward the basket on a fast break. They had one Cavs defender to beat. Iguodala attempted a layup. But James swooped in and knocked the ball away. His incredible block kept the game tied.

Then, with only 53 seconds to go, Irving nailed a three-pointer. That gave Cleveland the lead. With 11 seconds left, James sank a free throw to seal the win. The Cavaliers were champions!

James recorded a **triple-double** in Game 7. He was also named the NBA Finals Most Valuable Player (MVP).

James makes a huge block on Andre Iguodala of the Warriors during Game 7 of the 2016 NBA Finals.

The superstar already had two career NBA titles, but this one was different. This title was for his home city of Cleveland.

CHAPTER 2

STRAIGHT TO THE NBA

LeBron Raymone James was born on December 30, 1984. He grew up in Akron, Ohio, just a few miles south of Cleveland. When LeBron was eight years old, a football coach asked him to join his team. LeBron had never played football before. But he instantly became the team's star.

Akron, Ohio, is home to approximately 200,000 people.

Months later, LeBron tried basketball for the first time. He loved the game, and he practiced constantly. His hard work paid off. As a freshman, LeBron was already the best basketball player at his high school. He led St. Vincent-St. Mary to a state championship that year. He did it again as a sophomore.

LeBron was a scoring machine. But he could do more than shoot. Many **scouts** believed his best skill was passing. LeBron wasn't selfish with the ball. And that helped his teammates play better.

By LeBron's senior year, reporters from all over the United States were writing about him. St. Vincent-St. Mary even

James goes for a dunk during a 2002 high school game for St. Vincent-St. Mary.

moved its games to bigger arenas. That way, more people could watch LeBron play. Many of his games were also shown on national TV. He was a star, and he hadn't even finished high school yet.

James decided not to attend college. Instead, he headed straight to the NBA. The Cleveland Cavaliers selected him with the first pick in the 2003 NBA **Draft**.

Unfortunately for James, he was joining a lousy team. But he quickly helped turn things around. In 2006, Cleveland reached the playoffs for the first time

ROOKIE OF THE YEAR

The 2003 NBA Draft was loaded with talent. For example, Carmelo Anthony averaged 21 points per game as a **rookie**. Chris Bosh led all rookies in rebounds and blocks. But one player stood out from the pack. At the end of the 2003–04 season, LeBron James was named Rookie of the Year.

James drives against a Denver Nuggets defender in a 2003 game during his rookie season with the Cavaliers.

in years. And in 2007, the Cavs made it all the way to the Finals. However, James struggled in the series. The San Antonio Spurs **swept** the Cavs in four games. Cleveland's championship dreams would have to wait.

CHAPTER 3

THE DECISION

In his first five seasons, LeBron James showed that he was one of the best offensive players in the NBA. However, his defense wasn't great. That started to change during the 2008–09 season. James became one of the league's top defenders. He blocked shots, pulled down rebounds, and racked up steals.

James pulls down a rebound during a 2009 game against the Toronto Raptors.

These improvements made James a more complete player. In 2008–09, he led the Cavs to the NBA's best record. He also won his first MVP award. But despite the amazing season, Cleveland lost in the Eastern Conference finals.

The 2009–10 season unfolded in the same way. Once again, Cleveland had the best record in the league. Once again, James won the MVP award. And once again, the Cavs lost in the playoffs. It was a disappointing end to an otherwise fantastic season.

After the season was over, James had a big decision to make. His **contract** with the Cavaliers was ending. That meant

From left to right, Chris Bosh, Dwyane Wade, and James celebrate James's decision to join the Miami Heat.

he could join any team. James chose the Miami Heat. Superstars Dwyane Wade and Chris Bosh also played for the Heat. The trio looked unstoppable.

Fans in Cleveland were furious. They felt James had betrayed his hometown. Even so, James was ready for a change.

He thought the Heat would give him a better chance at winning a title.

In his first season with Miami, James led his team to the Finals. There, the Heat faced the Dallas Mavericks. Nearly everyone expected the Heat to win. James played well in Games 1 and 3. He helped

GIVING BACK

Even after James left the Cavaliers, he kept close ties with his home state. In particular, he continued supporting a charity that he'd started in Akron. This group focuses on keeping students in school. It also offers them **scholarships** so they can go to college. James believes education can help kids have better lives as adults.

James passes to a teammate during Game 5 of the 2011 NBA Finals.

Miami build a 2–1 lead in the series. But his play went downhill after that. In Game 4, James scored only eight points. Dallas ended up winning the series 4–2. James's quest for an NBA title had been denied yet again.

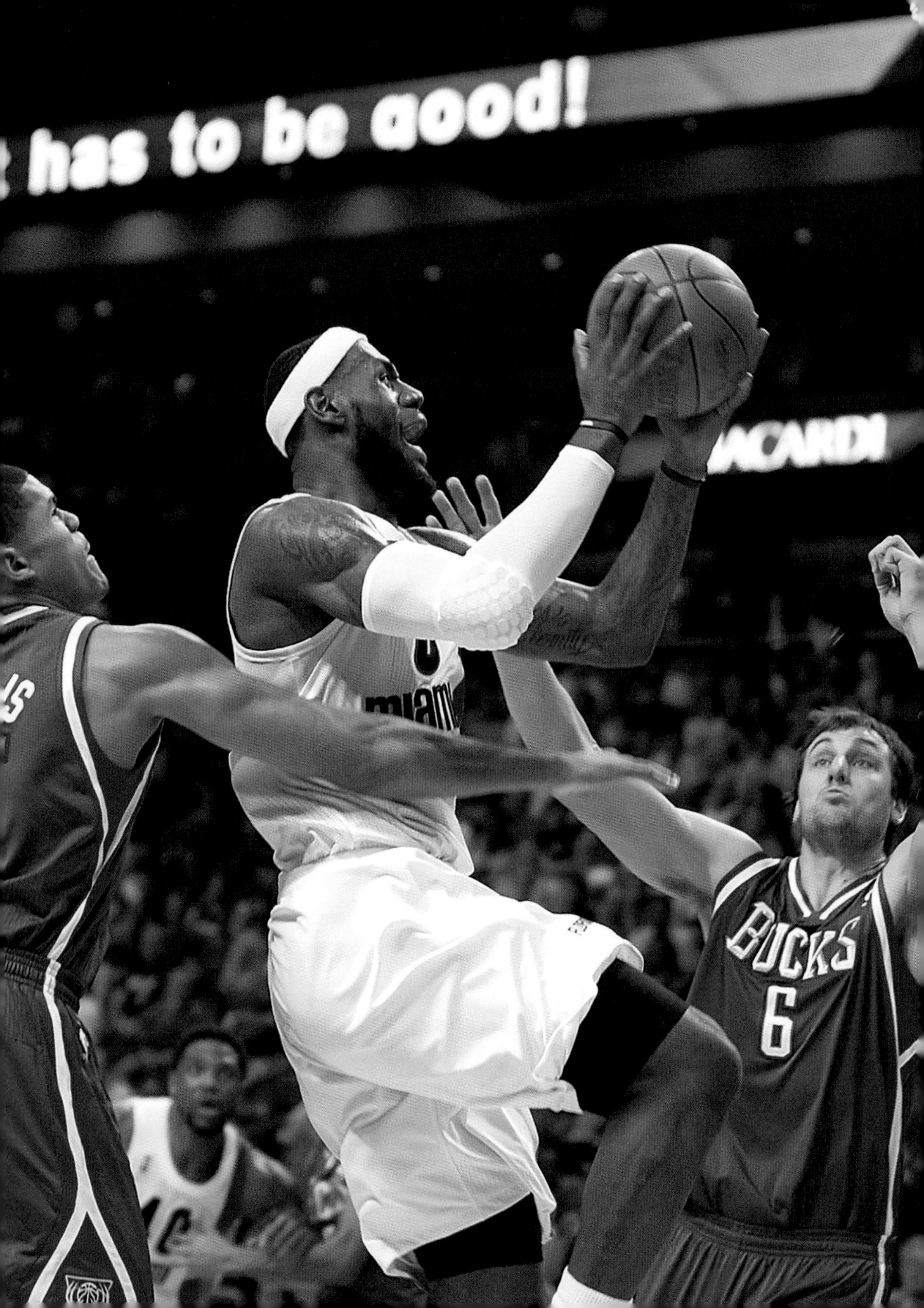
has to be good!
BUCKS
6

CHAPTER 4

CHAMPION AT LAST

After losing in the Finals for the second time, LeBron James started working harder than ever. In particular, he improved his skills in the **low post**. When the 2011–12 season rolled around, James played more aggressively near the basket. He led the Heat in scoring and won the third MVP award of his career.

James puts up a layup from the low post during a 2012 game against the Milwaukee Bucks.

More importantly, the Heat made it back to the Finals. They took on the Oklahoma City Thunder. After four games, Miami led the series 3–1. James wasn't going to let this one slip away. In Game 5, he recorded a triple-double. Miami crushed the Thunder 121–106. At last, James was an NBA champion.

After winning a title, James could have relaxed. But in 2012–13, James had one of his best seasons yet. He won another MVP award. And Miami claimed the league's top record. Best of all, James led his team to another championship.

The following season, the Heat came close to winning their third title in a row.

James posts up against James Harden of the Oklahoma City Thunder during Game 4 of the 2012 NBA Finals.

However, they fell to the San Antonio Spurs in the Finals.

James returned to the Cavaliers for the 2014–15 season. Cleveland was thrilled to have him back. The team reached the Finals that season. But the Golden State Warriors defeated the Cavs in six games.

In 2015–16, Cleveland finally had something to celebrate. James led the Cavs to a thrilling victory in Game 7 of the Finals. It was the first time the city of Cleveland had won a title in 52 years. The Cavs made it to the Finals again in the

MORE THAN A VOTE

James has often spoken out against racism and violence toward Black people. In May 2020, a Black man died in Minnesota after police pinned him to the ground. Protests spread across the country in response. James felt he had to respond, too. So, he started a group called More Than a Vote. This group aimed to increase Black voter turnout in the 2020 presidential election. It also worked against attempts to stop Black communities from voting.

James hits a fadeaway jumper against Ben Simmons of the Philadelphia 76ers during a 2020 game.

next two seasons. But both times, they lost to the Warriors.

In 2018, James joined the Los Angeles Lakers. And in 2020, he led the team to an NBA championship. It was the fourth title of his career. Basketball fans agreed that James was one of the greatest players of all time.

LeBRON JAMES

- Height: 6 feet 9 inches (206 cm)
- Weight: 250 pounds (113 kg)
- Birth date: December 30, 1984
- Birthplace: Akron, Ohio
- High school: St. Vincent-St. Mary High School (Akron, Ohio)
- NBA teams: Cleveland Cavaliers (2003–2010, 2014–2018); Miami Heat (2010–2014); Los Angeles Lakers (2018–)
- Major awards: NBA Rookie of the Year (2004); NBA All-Star (2005–2020); NBA MVP (2009, 2010, 2012, 2013); NBA champion (2012, 2013, 2016, 2020)

Los Angeles

Akron

Cleveland

Miami

FOCUS ON
LEBRON JAMES

Write your answers on a separate piece of paper.

1. Write a paragraph that explains the main ideas of Chapter 3.

2. Do you think James made the right choice when he left Cleveland in 2010? Why or why not?

3. When did James win his first MVP award?

> **A.** 2003
> **B.** 2009
> **C.** 2018

4. Why did James skip college?

> **A.** He didn't have the money to pay for it.
> **B.** No colleges wanted him on their teams.
> **C.** He was already good enough to play in the NBA.

Answer key on page 32.

GLOSSARY

contract
An agreement to pay someone a certain amount.

draft
A system that allows teams to acquire new players coming into a league.

elimination
A situation where a team loses a series and is knocked out of the playoffs.

low post
The area near the basket on a basketball court.

rookie
A professional athlete in his or her first year.

scholarships
Money given to students to pay for education expenses.

scouts
People who look for talented young players.

swept
Won all the games in a series.

triple-double
A game in which a player has double-digit numbers in three categories, often points, assists, and rebounds.

TO LEARN MORE

BOOKS

Fishman, Jon M. *LeBron James*. Minneapolis: Lerner Publications, 2018.

Howell, Brian. *LeBron James vs. Michael Jordan*. Minneapolis: Abdo Publishing, 2018.

Kelley, K. C. *Los Angeles Lakers*. Mankato, MN: The Child's World, 2019.

NOTE TO EDUCATORS

Visit **www.focusreaders.com** to find lesson plans, activities, links, and other resources related to this title.

INDEX

Answer Key: 1. Answers will vary; 2. Answers will vary; 3. B; 4. C